W9-AWY-126

The Art of Prayer

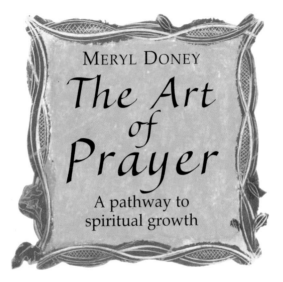

MERYL DONEY

The Art
of
Prayer

A pathway to
spiritual growth

DIMENSIONS
FOR LIVING

NASHVILLE

Dimensions for Living edition published 2001
First published by Lion Publishing plc
Sandy Lane West, Oxford, England

ISBN 0-687-09912-9

Cataloging-in-Publication data is available from the Library of Congress.

Acknowledgments

We would like to thank all those who have given us permission to include material in this book. Every effort has been made to trace and acknowledge copyright holders of all the quotations in this book. We apologize for any errors or omissions that may remain, and would ask those concerned to contact the publishers, who will ensure that full acknowledgment is made in the future.

Pages 9, 11, 35, 59, 61: Extracts taken from The New Revised Standard Version of the Bible, Anglicized Edition, copyright © 1989, 1995 by the Division of Christian Education of the National Council of the Churches of Christ in the United States of America, and used by permission. All rights reserved.

Pages 9, 22, 25: Extracts taken from the Good News Bible, published by the Bible Societies/HarperCollins Publishers Ltd, UK © American Bible Society 1966, 1971, 1976, 1992, used with permission.

Pages 11, 33, 39, 41, 44: Extracts taken from the *Holy Bible, New International Version*, copyright © 1973, 1978, 1984 by International Bible Society. Used by permission.

Page 58: Extract taken from the Authorized Version of the Bible (The King James Bible), the rights in which are vested in the Crown, and reproduced by permission of the Crown's Patentee, Cambridge University Press.

Page 61: Extract taken from The Revised Standard Version of the Bible, copyright © 1946, 1952, 1971 by the Division of Christian Education of the National Council of the Churches of Christ in the United States of America, and used by permission. All rights reserved.

01 02 03 04 05 06 07 08 09 10 — 10 9 8 7 6 5 4 3 2 1

Typeset in 8.75/11 Zapf Calligraphic
Printed and bound in Singapore

Contents

The ancient art of prayer

The joy of prayer is one of the best-kept secrets of the twentieth century. Our world relies on technology and on our ability to control the environment. As a result, we have tended to overlook something very basic to us as human beings: the need to know that we are not alone in the universe.

People have a natural instinct to reach out to whoever is 'out there' – the creator, the personality behind the universe, the one who is 'closer to us than breathing'. Even those who do not believe in any kind of god have probably prayed at some time in their lives.

And, after thousands of years of civilization, there are still millions who pray regularly.

You may have prayed when you were a child, at school or by your bed at night. You may have memories of feeling loved and cared for, of having someone to tell your worries to. And now you may be looking for something of that experience again.

This book is designed to share those well-kept secrets of prayer with anyone who would like to learn them. It draws most heavily on the Christian tradition of prayer, with all the insights gathered over 2,000 years of faith. However, the ideas here are equally valid for people of any or no religion. Prayer is a universal human activity, and one that can immeasurably enrich your life.

The simplest prayers

Prayer is communication. A baby's first sounds, for instance, are a form of prayer. 'Ma ma ma' – 'I want something, I need help.' And they are very effective. We rush to comfort the tiny individual.

Prayer is like that. We instinctively reach out to someone beyond ourselves, whether we think of that person as our creator, the one who set the universe in motion, or – as Jesus' own prayer, the Lord's Prayer, begins – as 'our Father' (and we might equally say 'our Mother', because God is beyond gender).

Prayer is one of the simplest forms of communication in the world. Because we are individual, thinking human beings, we often carry on conversations with ourselves inside our heads. In the same way, we can talk directly to God. We need not make it more complicated than that.

We use the words 'Oh God!' all the time. Whether we mean them as a prayer, or simply as an exclamation, they are a kind of leftover prayer from a more religious age. And simple words breathed towards God when we are in trouble or in need are still real prayers. They are sometimes called 'arrow' prayers because they are words shot straight from the heart.

Pictures of prayer

Each person's experience of prayer is individual to them, and it is therefore not easy to say exactly what prayer is. Sometimes using picture language can help. Here are some of the most well-known images of prayer.

Parent and child

Jesus referred to God as 'my Father', and his prayer in the Gospel of Matthew begins, 'Our Father in heaven'. In the same gospel, he also used the picture of a father giving good gifts to his children. 'Is there anyone among you who, if your child asks for bread, will give a stone?… How much more will your Father in heaven give good things to those who ask him!'

An Old Testament figure, Isaiah, gives the picture of God taking care of the nation of Israel like a mother. 'You will be like a child that is nursed by its mother, carried in her arms, and treated with love. I will comfort you in Jerusalem, as a mother comforts her child.'

These pictures may be problematic if you did not have a good relationship with your parents, or if they were largely absent during your childhood. However, to imagine that we are talking to the best of all possible parents is still a helpful way to think of God hearing our prayers.

Friends

Perhaps the image of friends talking together is more helpful. A good friend is someone who really understands, to whom we can tell anything. Prayer can be like this.

Lovers

When you love someone, you want to be with them all the time. Conversation is easy. You talk about every little thing. You share your past and plan the future. Often just being together, not talking, gazing at each other, is enough communication. There is a kind of prayer that is like this. Just being still with God is enough.

Nearer than breathing

Prayer has been described by James Montgomery as 'the Christian's vital breath'. What is closer to us than our own breath? Prayer involves slowing down and becoming conscious of our own breathing. God is as close to us as this, part of us, giving us life.

Sunbathing

A more unusual picture, used by Sister Wendy Beckett, is that prayer is like sunbathing in God's presence. This is a beautiful image of prayer without words. Everyone feels so much better when the sun comes out. The warmth lifts the spirits and suddenly nothing seems as bad as it was. Like the sun, God's presence warms the heart. We can bathe the spiritual side of ourselves in it.

The just judge

This image of prayer comes from a story Jesus told about a woman who took her case to a judge. In the story the judge was not a good judge, but the woman pestered him so much that he finally took on her case. Jesus pointed out that if a reluctant judge can be persuaded to act, then God, who is a truly fair judge, will certainly hear and help us when we ask for something. It can be a sobering but very comforting thought to know that when we ask God for something, we are coming to someone who is unfailingly fair and trustworthy.

Famous short prayers

What shall I do, Lord?

St Paul's response to seeing Jesus on the road to Damascus

God save the King!

This phrase is used not only as a prayer but as a loyal toast. It comes from the first book of Samuel in the Old Testament.

God bless this bunch as they munch their lunch.

A grace

May we who are sinners deserve our dinners.

Rabbi Lionel Blue's favourite grace

I'm tired, Lord, but I'll lift one foot if you'll lift the other for me.

Saidia Patterson

O Lord, that lends me life, lend me a heart replete with thankfulness.

William Shakespeare

Come, Lord Jesus!

From the book of Revelation in the New Testament

God bless us every one!

Tiny Tim in 'A Christmas Carol' by Charles Dickens

Different types of prayer

Many people have found it helpful to write down the different types of prayer as a list. In order to make them easy to remember, they have been grouped together to form the word **ACTS**.

A Adoration

Adoration means realizing who God is and offering worship.

Prayer often begins with words that express how great God is. This is not because God needs to be flattered like an emperor in ancient times. It is simply a natural human response when we talk to our creator.

C Contrition

Contrition means confessing and saying we are sorry for our mistakes and omissions.

They say that confession is good for the soul. When we approach God, we can sometimes feel a sense of failure because we don't measure up to his standards. It is hard to admit that we have done things wrong, or not done things that we should have done. But this can be the best part of prayer. Keeping short accounts with God, knowing that we are forgiven, is a great liberator. When things have gone wrong, confession and forgiveness can bring a fantastic feeling of release and the chance to start again.

T Thanksgiving

Thanksgiving means thanking God for everything that is good.

This, like adoration, should be a natural part of our conversation with God. If times are good – if we are happy or in a lovely place – we can express all these feelings, thanking God for the beauty of life. If you don't feel happy or thankful, on the other hand, thanksgiving is not an appropriate kind of prayer. You don't have to pretend to be thankful in order to please God.

It can, however, be helpful to stop and look around you when you come to pray, and to think about what you do enjoy. There's a lot to be said for the old saying 'count your blessings'. It can help to put things into perspective.

S Supplication

Supplication means asking God for things and praying for other people.

We don't usually need any prompting to ask God for things. In fact, our most basic instinct is to come to God when we want or need something. But this is as it should be. A parent is always glad when their child asks for help. There is no worse feeling than to be excluded from helping when we know that someone is in need.

Praying for other people is a good way of bringing other people to God. Sometimes it is the only thing we can do for them. And it can be a great comfort to be able to talk to God about the situation.

Jesus' model prayer

When one of his followers said to Jesus, 'Lord, teach us to pray,' his response was to give them an example prayer to follow. This prayer has become known as the Lord's Prayer, and people have been using it ever since. Today there are several translations in general use. This one may be familiar from your schooldays.

Our Father in heaven,   ADORATION
hallowed be your name,
your kingdom come,
your will be done,
on earth as in heaven.
Give us today our daily bread.   SUPPLICATION
Forgive us our sins   CONTRITION
as we forgive those who sin against us.
Lead us not into temptation   SUPPLICATION
but deliver us from evil.
For the kingdom, the power,   ADORATION
and the glory are yours
now and for ever.
Amen.

Prayer in your life

You don't need to change your life in order to fit prayer into it. Prayer can happen anywhere and at any time. The next few pages will give some idea of where to begin, what to say and how to say it. There may be some aspects of prayer that you are familiar with and some that are completely new. Try them out. Learn as you go along. The whole process should be one of experiment and discovery; remember, there is no such thing as a 'wrong prayer'.

You don't have to change your life to fit prayer into it – although you may well find that your life changes through becoming someone who prays!

Anywhere, any time

Anyone can pray to God, anywhere and at any time. C.S. Lewis, who wrote the *Narnia* books for children, remembers first becoming aware of the reality of God as he rode in the sidecar of a motorbike on the way to the zoo! You can begin anywhere you like. Just talk to God. There is no need to use formal language or the 'right' words.

And although God knows what is happening to us, what we are thinking and what we need before we even begin to pray, we are still invited to come and talk about it. That's the mystery of prayer.

How to begin

Find a quiet place or somewhere you can be alone. It could be your bedroom or a spare room. You might be able to drop into a church or place of worship, find a seat in the local park, sit in your car or go for a walk.

When you are ready, start talking to God about anything and everything.

Some ways to pray

When you pray, the position of your body is not fundamentally important. All that is needed is an inner turning to God, a conversation inside your head. But in another sense, the way you use your body is important. It expresses who you are in all kinds of subtle ways. We call it 'body language', and it is true that the body can speak just by a gesture or a look.

Hands together, eyes closed

There is no rule that says you must close your eyes to pray. It is probably done in order to cut down distractions and to aid concentration. Possibly children are told to put their hands together to stop them fidgeting!

The *orans*

One of the oldest postures for prayer is standing with arms raised and palms forward or turned upwards. Pictures of people praying in this way are sometimes called *orans* from the Latin word *orare*, to speak or pray. They have been found as far apart as ancient Egypt and early Christian Britain.

Kneeling

Kneeling to pray is found in many traditions, especially the Anglican Church. This may date back to the ancient custom of serfs kneeling before a master with their hands between his knees as a mark of respect.

Sitting

Many people sit to pray, either upright or bent forward with their face in their hands. As the fourteenth-century mystic Richard Rolle expressed it, 'I sat because I knew that I longer lasted than going, or standing or kneeling. For in sitting I am most at rest and my heart most upward.'

Prostration

It has long been the practice of priests, monks and nuns to pray lying face down on the floor, sometimes with their arms out in the shape of a cross. This might seem rather extreme in the modern world, but it can also be a very powerful picture of dependence upon God. The busy vicar's wife Joyce Huggett says, 'When I came to prayer exhausted, I would sometimes lie in this position and voice a simple prayer: "Lord, there are no words to express what I long to say to you. Please interpret the language of my body lying prostrate before you." '

A classic position

This is a classic position for meditation. The person sits cross-legged on the floor with the right foot on the left thigh and the left foot on the right thigh. The back of the right hand rests on the left foot and the left hand rests palm-up on top of the right hand, the tips of the thumbs just touching. The body is aligned so that the ears and shoulders, nose and navel are in line.

What to say

The beginning

There is no need to use any special words or formal greeting when you begin to pray. Use words that express the way you feel about God.

The Lord's Prayer begins 'Our Father…', and the word used could be translated 'daddy'. God is seen as a loving parent. You could say 'Father', or 'Mother', 'Dear God', 'O God', 'Creator God'… anything that feels right for you.

In the Christian tradition God is seen as one God but at the same time three distinct persons: the Father, Jesus the Son and the Holy Spirit. Some people prefer to talk to Jesus because he understands what it is like to be human; others pray to the Holy Spirit because they feel that as a spirit he or she can be close to them. One of the Spirit's names means 'the one who draws alongside to help'.

The middle

So begin where you are. Don't try to arrange your prayers in a special order. There is no 'right' form of prayer. If there is something that is particularly worrying you, begin with that. Tell God all about it.

On the other hand, stream-of-consciousness prayer can turn into one long worry session. You may find yourself going round and round thinking the same thoughts rather than praying. It can then be helpful to follow the types of prayer on page 12, to use the words of ready-made prayers or to try being quiet in God's presence.

The end

To end a prayer, many people use the word 'Amen'. This is Old English, from the Hebrew word for 'certainly', and simply means 'so be it' or 'I agree'. When used at the end of a prayer that is read out loud, it is a way of agreeing with what has been said and joining in the prayer.

The many names of God

Here are a few names for God, taken from the Jewish and Christian traditions.

FATHER	MOTHER
ABBA ('DEAR FATHER')	FRIEND
JESUS CHRIST	SUPREME BEING
MESSIAH	RULER OF THE UNIVERSE
HOLY SPIRIT	
GREAT SPIRIT	SUSTAINER OF CREATION
THE ETERNAL	EVERLASTING GOD
THE CREATOR	GOD OF ETERNITY

Asking for things

This is probably the most natural form of prayer of all. We turn to God when we are in need, when we want something, when we are at the end of our own resources. And that is how it should be.

The parent and child picture is helpful here. Parents usually know what their children need. They could provide everything for their children without talking to them about it, but they would lose out on a lot. Parents are happy when their children come to them and ask for what they need. It's what they are there for! Certainly, they may have to say 'no' on occasions, but that's all part of the healthy relationship between them.

In the Gospel of Matthew, Jesus said, 'Ask, and you will receive; seek, and you will find; knock, and the door will be opened to you.'

Praying for others

When we care about our friends and the people we are involved with, we may want to talk to God about them. And when they are in need and we have done all that is humanly possible to help them, it is possible to do one thing more: pray for them.

Sometimes we know what we want to ask God to do. The issues are clear-cut. However, more often it is just a case of talking to God about what is going on and asking for help for the person. Often we don't know what is best for them anyway. But we can confidently ask God to do what is right for them.

Sometimes it is enough to mention people's names in prayer to God. Some people collect photos of their friends, to prompt their memory when they pray. Others keep a prayer notebook. This might include a list of those you wish to remember regularly, such as close family and friends, people you work with or members of a group or club. It could also list any situations, places, organizations, groups of people or even countries that you specially care about. The very organized may even make lists of things to pray for on different days of the week and on special dates. Extra space can be included in which to note down specific needs and to add updates as circumstances change.

Sorting things out

Oddly enough, one of the first reactions we may have when we begin to pray is to feel guilty. Thinking about God can remind us of all the things we have done wrong or failed to do. This reaction is quite normal. None of us is perfect. We have all thought, said and done things that we are not happy about.

If you lie to a friend, for instance, you feel bad about it. And it begins to spoil the relationship between you. Usually there is only one way to rescue the situation: to own up. Then it's up to the friend. They can forgive you and put things right, or refuse and leave the situation unresolved.

In the same way, the things we do wrong can spoil our relationship with God. If we don't deal with this situation we can feel cut off from God and unable to pray.

There is a way round this, and it is called confession. We can muster up our courage and own up – tell God all about it and ask to be forgiven. And we can always be forgiven when it is God we have offended. God doesn't want the friendship to be broken any more than we do.

Making amends

The first result of knowing we have been forgiven by God can be a feeling of joy and relief. But we may also feel the need to make amends for what has gone wrong. This might mean apologizing to someone, or doing some forgiving of our own. This can be a really worthwhile thing to do, though very hard at times.

Practical as ever, in the Gospel of Matthew Jesus put it like this: 'If you are about to offer your gift to God at the altar and there you remember that your brother has something against you, leave your gift there in front of the altar, go at once and make peace with your brother, and then come back and offer your gift to God.'

Talking about it

People who are still worried by feelings of guilt may wish to talk to someone else about it. Many churches offer confession and counselling as a practical help in these circumstances. Just as they would go to a doctor to talk about their physical symptoms if they were not well, so they might wish to talk to a priest or vicar who is trained to recognize the symptoms of an unhappy spiritual life.

Saying thank you

If you are happy, if something good has happened or if you are in a beautiful place, tell God about it. Express your feelings. Give thanks where you believe they are due.

An old children's song goes:

Count your blessings,
name them one by one,
and it will surprise you
what the Lord has done!

It is good to take stock of all the positive things in our lives from time to time. This can prevent us from being overwhelmed by problems and the general gloom often brought on by the daily news.

This poem by Gerard Manley Hopkins sums up his feeling of joy and thankfulness for creation.

Glory be to God for dappled things –
for skies of couple-colour as a brinded cow;
for rose-moles all in stipple upon trout that swim;
fresh-firecoal chestnut-falls; finches' wings;
landscape plotted and pierced-fold, fallow, and plough;
and all trades, their gear and tackle and trim.
All things counter, original, spare, strange;
whatever is fickle, freckled (who knows how?)
with swift, slow; sweet, sour; adazzle, dim;
he fathers-forth whose beauty is past change:
praise him.

Prayer at work

As these prayers show, every area of life can be brought to God in prayer.

A circuit judge

Dear Lord,
please give me
the Wisdom
the Energy
the Time
to do this job properly.

Christopher Compston

A consultant in mathematics education

Lord , when I am tempted to make myself indispensable, grant me the grace and common sense to make myself redundant.

Phil Boorman

A gardener

Lord, grant that I may live to be
steadfast and patient as a tree,
with roots held firm while branches bend
whate'er the trials on me descend.

David Gray

A homemaker

Lord, here I stand swirling the soapsuds,
watching the dirt disappear,
seeing the sunlight held in the bubbles.
I reflect, Lord, that this is how you deal with me,
pouring your love into my life,
living water, washing away the dirt, the sin,
filling me with the radiance of light.
Lord, keep me swirling.

Dorothy Jamal

An angler

Give me, O Lord, to catch a fish
so large that even I
in boasting of it afterwards
shall have no need to lie.

Lancelot Fleming

Praying with the senses

One of the good things about living in the
late twentieth century is the fact that we are
far more in touch with our feelings than we
used to be. And that goes for men as well
as women. Particularly in the areas of
spirituality and religion, the fact that we
have five senses tended to be forgotten.
Only the mind seemed to be used.

Here are some ideas that will bring all
the senses into prayer. Each can add richness
to the experience.

Getting in touch

The way your regular prayer place feels is important. You may not be able to find anywhere you can make into your own space, but it is still a good idea to think about where you choose and to make it as special as possible.

Make sure it is a place in which you can be relaxed and comfortable and not worry about interruptions. If you are easily distracted, keep it plain and simple. If you have a tendency to fall asleep as soon as you sit down, keep it cool and use pictures and colours to turn your mind to prayer (see page 36). If you need to calm down and lower your stress levels, make it warm and relaxing.

Posture is important, too (see page 18). If you sit to pray, find a good seat, not too hard and uncomfortable – nor too soft, or you may be tempted to drop off to sleep! If you kneel, have something supportive to kneel on. Sitting cross-legged on the floor can be tough, but aids concentration.

None of these things is essential, but thinking about them can help you to make the most of your prayer time.

A sweet-smelling offering

Today we use flowers, incense sticks, potpourri and perfumed oils to make our homes a pleasure to live in. There is no reason why we should not also use fragrances as an aid to prayer.

Perfumed incense has traditionally been used in worship in all the world's major religions. In Old Testament times it was burned as part of the temple worship. The sweet smell was an image of the beauty of God's presence, and the smoke drifting upwards symbolized the prayers of the people.

You might like to add the dimension of perfume to the place where you pray. Light a scented candle or an incense burner before you begin. Keep a scented plant or a bowl of potpourri in the room.

The meaning of perfumes

FRANKINCENSE

This is a gum collected from the Boswellia tree. It gives off a sweet scent when warmed or burned. It was used as incense for worship in Bible times, and was one of the gifts brought by the wise men to Jesus.

ROSEMARY

This herb has a lingering perfume, and is usually associated with the act of remembrance. It also symbolizes protection and the fidelity of lovers, and is therefore included in wedding bouquets.

LILY OF THE VALLEY

One of the first flowers of the year, this little flower with its overwhelming perfume heralds the return of spring. It is therefore associated with the coming of Christ, the season of Advent. It is also linked with Christ through an interpretation of the verse in the Song of Songs, 'I am a rose of Sharon, a lily of the valleys.'

THYME

'This herb the wise Lord made holy in the heavens; he let it down, placed it and sent it into the seven worlds as a cure for all, the poor and the rich.'

Anonymous

A taste of paradise

It might seem strange to use the sense of taste in worship. But there is no reason why not. There is a psalm in the Bible that says, 'O taste and see that the Lord is good.' Certainly our food is something for which we happily give thanks, and a sense of taste is a great gift.

A cup of tea or coffee taken with you to your prayer place might be a good way of getting in touch with how you are feeling. As you drink, you can thank God for the good things in life.

This is a prayer written by Richard Foster, the author of several books on prayer.

Somehow, Jesus, I like praying with a cup of coffee in my hands. I guess the warmth of the cup settles me and speaks of the warmth of your love. I hold the cup against my cheek and listen, hushed and still. I blow on the coffee and drink. Spirit of God, blow across my little life and let me drink in your great life.

Seeing is believing

What can you see when you get to your prayer place?
Does the dust on the windowsill remind you that you
haven't got around to cleaning yet? Can you see into your
neighbour's garden, where she is tending the best show
of flowers in the road? Are the walls painted a depressing
brown? All these things can take your mind off prayer.

You may be able to do simple things to eliminate some
of these distractions. Colours can make a real difference
to your thoughts and feelings. If you can't paint walls,
you might be able to pin up a piece of fabric.

Something to look at can help you to concentrate. A
candle which you light when you begin to pray, a bowl of
flowers (adding perfume as well), a picture of a beautiful
place, a cross – use anything which has meaning for you.

As a last resort, you can always shut your eyes and
imagine yourself anywhere in the world.

Praying with icons

The Eastern Christian church has always used pictures as
an aid to worship. They are called icons, from the Greek
word for image. Some people have criticized this practice.
They fear that people might worship the picture itself.
However, the Eastern belief has always been that to look at
an icon is to look beyond the picture and to respond to the
person pictured there. Icons are not portraits but pictures
of great spiritual truth, and can help towards prayer.

Listening in

You may not be able to arrange for absolute silence, but what you hear can be important in prayer. You could begin by listening to the sounds around you. If they're beautiful, like a blackbird singing, they will be easy to thank God for. If they're awful – if you can hear the neighbours fighting, for instance – you can talk to God about it.

Try using a piece of music to create an atmosphere or mood before you begin to pray. If you are the sort of person who finds total silence uncomfortable or distracting, you could play ambient music throughout your prayer time. A song can focus the mind, and if you are a musician you might play something yourself as part of your prayer. Speaking poetry or reading prayers out loud can help to bring home the meaning of the words.

Don't be afraid of silence, however. It can be a real discipline simply to be quiet for a short length of time. Inner silence is an even more difficult thing to achieve, but it is one of the skills of prayer. There's more about this on page 41.

A moment of calm

Prayers to help you stop, think and pray wherever you are.

O make my heart so still, so still,
when I am deep in prayer,
that I might hear the white mist-wreaths
losing themselves in air!

Utsonomya San, Japan

Drop thy still dues of quietness
till all our strivings cease,
take from our souls the strain and stress,
and let our ordered lives confess
the beauty of thy peace.

John Greenleaf Whittier

When you dwell on the sound of your breathing,
when you can really hear it coming and going,
peace will not be far behind.

Paul Wilson

Lord, temper with tranquillity
our manifold activity,
that we may do our work for thee
with very great simplicity.

Ascribed to a medieval monk

Be still, and know that I am God.

From the Old Testament book of Psalms

Going deeper

Prayer can express a very simple relationship
with God. But, as with any relationship,
there are always deeper levels to be explored
and enjoyed. Over the last 2,000 years there
have been many men and women of deep
faith who have set out on the adventure of
prayer, and there is a rich store of wisdom
in the prayers they wrote. Some of the ideas
in the next few pages are based on these
insights.

Learning to listen

Prayer doesn't have to be all talk. Many of the Christian mystics wrote about learning the art of being quiet, meditating and listening to God.

First, find a quiet place in which to pray. You may need to close your eyes in order not to be distracted by the things around you. If you have children who are crying or if the phone is ringing, there's no way in which you will be able to listen to God. Deal with those things first – and if they mean that you can't take time to pray at the moment, well, so be it. Life's like that.

When you have managed to grab a quiet moment, there is still the problem of inner noise: the thousand and one voices that clamour for attention. Suddenly we become aware of the things that must be done urgently, the people who need us and the good things waiting to be enjoyed. These thoughts are always with us, and can get in the way of listening to God. One way to deal with this is to take a moment to write everything down in a notebook. Then consciously put them to the back of your mind while you concentrate on God.

The next step is to find your own way into listening. Try looking at a picture or an object like a candle or a flower. Or you might prefer to repeat some words over and over again, like these from the Psalms: 'Be still, and know that I am God,' or the Jesus Prayer (see page 45).

When you are quiet and still, outwardly and inwardly, you are ready to listen. Ask God to speak to you.

Meditation

Meditation means to think deeply about something, and is practised in many of the world's religions. Christians have always viewed the Bible, both the Old and New Testaments, as one of the ways in which God speaks to people. St Ignatius Loyola taught a special method of meditating on the Bible. It is designed to bring the story to life for the reader so that the words and ideas can become part of his or her life.

Choose a story or a short passage from the Bible. (It will help if you understand some of the context of what you are reading: who it is about, what happens before and afterwards. A Bible with study notes in it may be useful.) Read it through several times, very slowly, a phrase or verse at a time. As you read, try to imagine yourself there. See the events happen in front of you. Think about what you can see, hear, feel – even smell! As the events unfold, enter into it with your imagination and notice how you feel.

When you have finished reading, think about it and allow the main points to sink into your mind. Ask yourself what God might be saying to you personally through this story. Does it change the way you see things? Does it help you to understand anything better?

A meditation like this often ends in prayer as you talk to God about what you have heard, seen and experienced.

Spiritual reading

Lecto divina is a Latin expression meaning 'spiritual reading'. It has been described as 'reading with the mind in the heart'. It is similar to Ignatius' meditation, but includes reading the passage slowly and praying as you go along, making the experience a form of conversation.

Know yourself

Ignatius also described a method of prayer called the *examen* or 'examination of conscience'. It comes from the Latin word for the indicator that marks weight accurately on a pair of scales.

In this form of prayer, our motives and actions are opened up to God, and we ask for an accurate assessment of our lives from God's point of view. This can be a painful process. We talk about our conscience 'pricking' us, and sometimes that's how it feels. Yet God's attitude to us is one of love and concern. Like a mother who gently removes a splinter from her child's finger, she must hurt in order to help her child.

Ignatius recommended using the Ten Commandments from the Old Testament as a way of checking out our behaviour and attitudes. Or you may prefer to use Jesus' summary of the commandments in the Gospel of Matthew.

Love the Lord your God with all your heart
and with all your soul and with all your mind.
Love your neighbour as yourself.

Go over these two sentences slowly. Ask yourself if you measure up to this high ideal. Talk to God about it.

The prayer of the heart

There is an ancient Christian prayer, developed among the Eastern Orthodox churches, known as the Jesus Prayer. It springs from a story Jesus told about a religious person of the time – a Pharisee – and a sinner. In the story, the Pharisee prays to God with pride in his heart, but the sinner calls out, 'God, be merciful to me, a sinner!'

The Jesus Prayer has been called a Christian mantra, but this is slightly misleading. The prayer is not meant to be repeated as a means to meditation, but slowly and reverently as a conscious prayer to Jesus.

Lord Jesus Christ,
have mercy on me.

The prayer is repeated slowly in rhythm with the breathing – in for the first line and out for the second. Its aim is to bring the person praying to a level of *hesuchia* or stillness: when you can rest in God without talking or thinking. This is sometimes called 'the prayer of the heart'.

Prayers from the media

Prayer is an experience we have in common with all people. Some of the most moving scenes in recent films and musicals have included moments of prayer.

Oh, watch the day
once again hurry off,
and the sun bathe
itself in the water.
The time for us to rest approaches.
Oh God, who dwelleth in heavenly light,
who reigns above in heaven's hall,
be for us our infinite light
in the valley of the night.
The sand in our hour-glass will soon run out.
The day is conquered by the night.
The glares of the world are ending,
so brief their day, so swift their flight.
God, let thy brightness ever shine.
Admit us to thy mercy divine.

An evening prayer from the film 'Babette's Feast'

O most merciful redeemer,
may I know thee more clearly,
love thee more dearly,
follow thee more nearly,
day by day.

*This prayer, written by Richard of Chichester in the
thirteenth century, forms the basis for the song 'Day
by Day' from the musical 'Godspell'.*

Lord, who made the lion and the lamb –
you decreed I should be what I am.
Would it spoil some vast, eternal plan
if I were a wealthy man?

Tevye's prayer from the film 'Fiddler on the Roof'

How prayer can help

Prayer is not the answer to all our problems. God has never promised to make life easy or smooth for us, just to be there with us in all the ups and downs. And being available to hear our prayers and understand our longings, needs and joys is of more help than we can measure.

Here are a few pointers to ways in which we can approach God in prayer in both the good times and the bad.

When hard times come

When life gets tough, when things go wrong and we feel
lonely, trapped, worried and at the end of our tether, we
can still pray. And it is important to be honest in prayer.
There's no point in pretending anything to God, who
knows the situation in far more detail than we do. Richard
Foster says, 'In the same way that a small child cannot
draw a bad picture, so a child of God cannot offer a bad
prayer.'

So, if all our hopes have come crashing down around
our ears, we can pace the floor with God, telling our
father, our mother all about it. If life has been unfair to us,
we can feel free to complain to God, to argue, even to yell
and scream. We'll be in good company. The Old Testament
prophets did that quite often.

Above all, don't try to second-guess what God wants
to hear. Just say what you want.

In bereavement and loss

Strangely enough, it can be very hard to pray when someone we love is ill or dies. This is not an unusual experience. At such times the most manageable thing is to be still and quiet in front of God, not trying to talk at all. This, too, is a form of prayer.

It can also be a time when we let other people pray for us. We can draw strength and support from the fact that God's love surrounds us whatever we are going through.

It is very important to be able to talk to people about the person we have lost. It can be a real help in working through our feelings and coming to terms with the bereavement. Friends, of course, are not always with us at the crucial moments – but God is always there.

Shakespeare expressed it like this in *Macbeth*.

Give sorrow words.
The grief that does not speak
whispers the o'erfraught heart,
and bids it break.

This prayer is a simple cry from the heart.

O God,
in the darkness,
hear me.
Meryl Doney

Life's special occasions

It is traditional to include prayers in the great events of our lives – weddings, baptisms, funerals – and when people get together in groups such as school assemblies or state occasions.

We instinctively mark moments of change by throwing a party, spring-cleaning the house, buying new clothes or having a special meal. In the same way, more and more people are wanting to mark some of the other, more personal events in their lives with rituals or ceremonies that make them special. A good new anthology of prayers will include words for such events as welcoming a baby home, a house-warming, a blessing for an adoption, when a family emigrates and for the end of a relationship.

You could write your own prayers for these events in your life. There are some ideas for this on page 54.

Good Lord!

Prayer doesn't have to be serious all the time. After all, God invented humour.

Dear Lord,
please put your arm
round my shoulder
and your hand
over my mouth.
Prayer of an American woman

O Lord, grant that we may
not be like porridge, stiff,
stodgy and hard to stir,
but like cornflakes, crisp,
fresh and ready to serve.
Lancelot Fleming

Oh God, make me good,
but not yet.
St Augustine of Hippo

Good Lord,
please help my unbelief.
You really do exist?
Good lord!
Charles Brien

Please make
bad people good
and good people nice.
Child's prayer

From silly devotions
and from sour-faced saints
good Lord, deliver us.
St Teresa of Avila

Your own book of prayers

Books of prayers can be very helpful. They can inspire you to pray in new ways and give you well-chosen words for special occasions. But there may come a time when you want to write a prayer of your own. It might be a family occasion which needs a special grace or blessing, or it could be some prayers for you to use in your own life.

Here are some ideas on writing prayers and making your own collection of 'classics'.

Prayers for special occasions

Those who have attempted to write prayers have quickly realized that it is not as easy as it looks. In fact, because prayers for use in public have to be short and sound good when read aloud, preparing them is probably nearer to writing poetry than anything else. It may help to look at a few prayers to see how they are written.

To begin with, write down roughly what you want to say and the points you need to cover. Then group them so that one idea leads on to the next. Try to say something about each idea, but keep the lines short.

Think about the people who will join in the prayer with you. This is important in deciding what to say and how to begin the prayer. It can simply be 'O God', or 'Our Father', but you could also add a line to link the prayer to the occasion, such as 'O God, who made us to live in families…' A more formal prayer might need a special ending, so that people can say 'Amen' to express their agreement. If it is to be a Christian prayer, a traditional close might be 'through Jesus Christ our Lord'. A more general wording might be 'in God's holy name'.

Before you finish, try out your prayer by reading it aloud slowly. Make sure that the thoughts are clearly understandable and that the words run easily off the tongue.

Personal prayers

If the prayer is for your own private use, you can be much freer in what you say and how you express it. For example, you may want to write a prayer for your family that you can use regularly. You could then name each family member, including something that you specially want to say about them, things you like about them or worries they may have.

Finish off the prayer with one of the well-known formulas or by using your own words, including 'Amen' if you wish.

Haiku prayer

Writing prayers is close to writing poetry. Here is an example of a prayer written using a traditional form of Japanese poetry known as a *haiku*. It has three lines, the first with five syllables, the second seven and the third five.

Go into the world
with a daring and tender love.
The world is waiting.

Women's Conference, Japan

Collecting classics

There are thousands of prayers published in collections and used all around the world. Many have been handed down throughout the history of the Christian church, and some have become classics.

You may like to keep a notebook in which you write down prayers you like and want to use regularly. Here are a few of the most well-known.

The shepherd psalm

This prayer is taken from the King James version of Psalm 23, probably the most famous psalm in the Bible.

The Lord is my shepherd; I shall not want.
He maketh me to lie down in green pastures:
he leadeth me beside the still waters.
He restoreth my soul: he leadeth me in the paths
of righteousness for his name's sake.
Yea, though I walk through the valley of the shadow
of death, I will fear no evil: for thou art with me;
thy rod and thy staff they comfort me.
Thou preparest a table before me in the presence
of mine enemies: thou anointest my head with oil;
my cup runneth over.
Surely goodness and mercy shall follow me all the
days of my life: and I will dwell in the house of the
Lord for ever.

A few lines from this prayer can be used as an 'arrow' prayer (see page 8).

(see page 8)

> The Lord is my shepherd,
> I shall fear nothing.

Mary's song

This prayer comes from a song which Mary sang when she knew that she was expecting her son Jesus. It can be found in the Gospel of Luke and is sometimes called the 'Magnificat', from the word 'magnifies'.

> My soul magnifies you, my Lord,
> and my spirit rejoices in God my Saviour,
> for you have looked with favour
> on the lowliness of your servant…
> You, the Mighty One, have done great things for me,
> and holy is your name.
> Your mercy is for those who fear you
> from generation to generation.
> You have scattered the proud in the thoughts
> of their hearts.
> You have brought down the powerful
> from their thrones,
> and lifted up the lowly;
> You have filled the hungry with good things,
> and sent the rich away empty.

The prayer of St Francis of Assisi

Lord, make me an instrument of your peace.
Where there is hatred, let me sow love;
where there is injury, pardon;
where there is discord, union;
where there is doubt, faith;
where there is despair, hope;
where there is darkness, light;
where there is sadness, joy.

O Divine Master, grant
that I may not so much seek
to be consoled as to console;
to be understood as to understand;
to be loved, as to love;
for it is in giving that we receive,
it is in pardoning that we are pardoned,
and it is in dying that we are born to eternal life.

Your prayer collection

You might like to make short selections of prayers written
by yourself and others to use at specific times. It is rather
like making a compilation tape of your favourite songs.
Here are some examples of morning prayers.

My Father, for another night
of quiet sleep and rest,
for all the joy of morning light,
your holy name be blest.

Henry William Baker

As you take a cup of tea to your quiet place:

O taste and see that the Lord is good.

From the Old Testament book of Psalms

As you look out at what sort of day it is:

This is the day which the Lord has made;
I will rejoice and be glad in it.

Adapted from the Old Testament book of Psalms

Think quietly over what has to be done today. Make
notes if it helps to keep you from getting sidetracked
into practical details. Then pray:

O Lord, into your hands I commit this day.
Be with me at every moment,
keep me from harm,
prompt me to do what is right,
and be what you want me to be.
To your praise and glory.
Amen.

Meryl Doney

Go in peace, to love and serve the Lord.

From The Alternative Service Book 1980

Further reading

Listening to God, Joyce Huggett (Trafalgar Square)

Prayer: Finding the Heart's True Home, Richard Foster (HarperSanFrancisco)

A Prayer Treasury (Chariot Victor Publishing)

A Time to Pray: 365 Classic Prayers to Help You Through the Year (Dimensions for Living)

A Time to Reflect: 365 Classic Meditations to Help You Through the Year (Dimensions for Living)

Heal My Heart, O Lord: Words from God for Healing and Hope, Joan Hutson (Dimensions for Living)

Acknowledgments

Pages 11, 29: 'A Sinner's Grace' and 'A Fisherman's Prayer' taken from *A Patchwork of Blessings and Graces*, Mary Daniels, copyright © 1996 Gracewing Ltd. Used by permission.

Page 14: The Lord's Prayer in its modern form as printed in *The Alternative Service Book 1980* is adapted from the version prepared by the International Consultation on English Texts (ICET) and is reproduced by permission of The Central Board of Finance of the Church of England.

Page 19: Extract taken from *Listening to God*, Joyce Huggett, copyright © 1996 and reproduced by permission of Hodder and Stoughton Ltd.

Pages 28, 29, 53: Extracts by Christopher Compston, Phil Boorman, David Gray, Dorothy Jamal and Charles Brien taken from *The 'Times' Book of Prayers*, Mowbray, copyright © 1997 individual contributors. Used by permission.

Page 35: Extract taken from *Prayers from the Heart*, Richard Foster, copyright © 1994 and reproduced by permission of Hodder and Stoughton Ltd.

Page 38: Extract taken from *The Little Book of Calm*, Paul Wilson, copyright © 1996 Pearls of Wilson, Penguin Books Australia Ltd. Used by permission.

Page 46: Extract taken from *Babette's Feast and Other Anecdotes of Destiny*, Isak Dinesen. Copyright © 1953, 1958 by Isak Dinesen. Copyright renewed 1981, 1986 by Isak Dinesen. Reprinted by permission of Vintage Books, a division of Random House, Inc.

Page 47: 'If I Were A Rich Man': lyric by Sheldon Harnick, copyright © 1964 by Alley Music Co. Inc. and Trio Music Co. Inc. Copyright renewed 1992 by Jerry Bock and Sheldon Harnick. All rights reserved. Lyric reproduction by kind permission of Carlin Music Corp., Iron Bridge House, 3 Bridge Approach, London NW1 8BD for the Commonwealth of Nations (including Hong Kong but excluding Canada and Australasia) and Eire.

Page 53: Extract taken from *A Book of Graces*, Carolyn Martin, copyright © 1996 Carolyn Martin and reproduced by permission of Hodder and Stoughton Ltd.

Page 56: Extract taken from a benediction by the 1984 Women's Conference in *Haiku, Origami, and More* by Judith May Newton and Mayumi Tabuchi, copyright © 1991 Friendship Press, Inc. Used by permission.

Page 62: Material from *The Alternative Service Book 1980* is copyright © The Central Board of Finance of the Church of England 1980 and is reproduced by permission.